THE BIG BOOK OF SMASH HITS!

This publication is not authorised for sale in the
United States of America and/or Canada.

WISE PUBLICATIONS
London/New York/Sydney/Paris/Copenhagen/Madrid/Tokyo

AMERICAN PIE

Words & Music by Don McLean

HAMPSHIRE COUNTY COUNCIL
County Library

100%
recycled paper

T

A tempo ♩=104

1. Did you— write the book of love— and do you— have faith in God a-bove?—
(Verse 2 see block lyric)

If the Bi-ble tells— you so.— Now do you— be-lieve— in

rock and roll— and can mu-sic save your— mor-tal soul, and can you teach— me

3

how to dance ___ real slow? _____ Well I

know that you're in love with him ___ coz I saw you danc-in' in the gym. ___ You

both kicked off your shoes. ___ Man I dig those rhy-thm and blues.
(Both kicked off your shoes. ___)

___ I was a lone-ly teen-age bronc-in' buck with a pink car-na-tion and a

pick-up truck. But I knew that I was out___ of luck___ the day___

___ the mu - - sic died.___ I start-ed sing-ing

bye - bye Miss A - me - ri - can Pie. Drove my Che-vy to the lev-ee but the

lev-ee was dry. Them good ole___ boys___ were drink-in' whis-ky and rye sing-in'

5

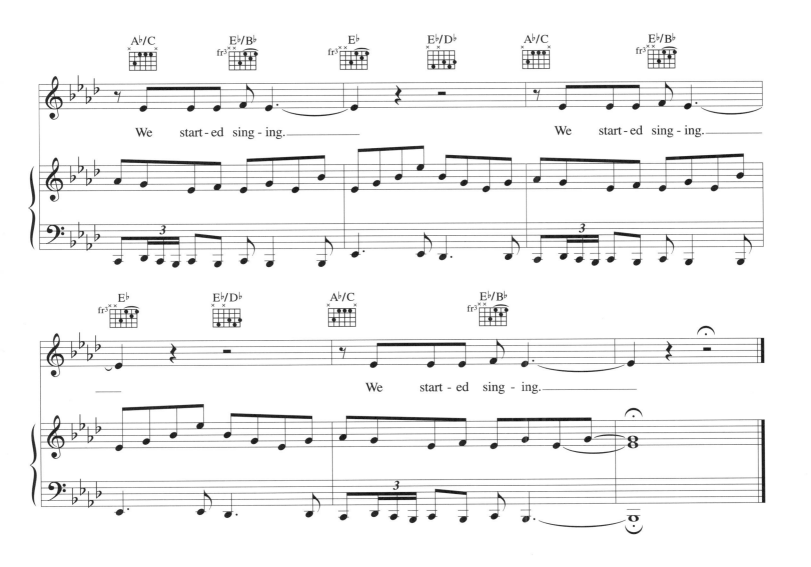

Verse 2:
I met a girl who sang the blues
And I asked her for some happy news
But she just smiled and turned away
Well I went down to the sacred store
Where I'd heard the music years before
But the man there said the music wouldn't play
Well now in the streets the children screamed
The lovers cried and the poets dreamed
But not a word was spoken
The church bells all were broken
And the three men I admire the most
The Father, Son and the Holy Ghost
They caught the last train for the coast
The day the music died
We started singing.

Bye-bye Miss American Pie *etc.*

BABYLON
Words & Music by David Gray

1. Fri - day night— an' I'm go - in' no - where, all the lights— are chan - gin' green—
(Verse 2 see block lyric)

jea-lous-y,___ that bit-ter-ness,___ that___ ri-di-cule.

An' if you want___ it, come an' get___ it, for cry-in' out___ loud.

___ The love that I___ was giv-in' you___ was

nev-er in___ doubt.___ Let go your heart,

let go your head___ and feel it___ now.

Let go your heart,___ let go your head___ and feel it___

1.

___ now, Ba - by - lon.___ Ba - by - lon.

2.

___ now.___

Let go your heart, ___ let go your head ___ and feel ___

___ it. Let go your heart, ___ let go your head ___

___ and feel it ___ now, _____ Ba - by - lon.

Ba - by - lon. ___

Con pedale

Ba - by - lon. _____

Ba - by - lon.

Ba - by - lon. _____

Why,

why, why, why, _ why, why? _____

N.C.

Verse 2:
Saturday an' I'm runnin' wild
An' all the lights are changin' red to green
Movin' through the crowds, I'm pushin'
Chemicals are rushin' in my bloodstream
Only wish that you were here
You know I'm seein' it so clear
I've been afraid to show you how I really feel
Admit to some o' those bad mistakes I've made.

Well, if you want it come an' get it *etc.*

BEAUTIFUL DAY

Music by U2
Lyrics by Bono

out of this place. Some-one you could lend a hand in re-

-turn for grace. It's a beau-ti-ful day.

The sky falls. And you feel like it's a beau-ti-ful day.

Don't let it get a-way. 2. You're on the road

Touch me, take me to that oth-er place.

Teach me, I know I'm not a hope-less case.

See the world in green and blue.— See Chi-na right— in front of you.

To Coda ⊕

See the can-yons brok-en by cloud. See the tu-na fleets clear-ing the sea out.

See the Bed-ouin fires at night. See the oil fields at first light

see the bird with a leaf in her mouth. Af-ter the flood all the col-ours came out.

D.%. al Coda

ad lib.

It was a beau-ti-ful

19

Verse 2:
You're on the road but you've got no destination
You're in the mud, in the maze of her imagination
You love this town even if that doesn't ring true
You've been all over and it's been all over you.

It's a beautiful day
Don't let it get away
It's a beautiful day
Don't let it get away.

On 𝄋:
It was a beautiful day
A beautiful day
Don't let it get away.

Touch me, take me to that other place
Reach me, I know I'm not a hopeless case.

BLACK COFFEE

Words & Music by Tom Nichols, Alexander Soos & Kirsty Elizabeth

Each mo-ment is new.____ Freeze__ the mo-

-ment.____ Each mo-ment is cool.____

Freeze__ the mo - ment.____ I

would-n't wan-na be a-ny-where__ else__ but here.____

24

25

Repeat ad lib. to fade

Verse 2:
Day dreaming, chain smoking
Always laughing, always joking
I remain the same
Did I tell you that I love you?
Brush your teeth and pour a cup
Of black coffee out
I love to watch you do that everyday
The little things that you do
Each moment is new
Freeze the moment
Each moment is cool
Freeze the moment.

I wouldn't wanna be anywhere else but here *etc.*

BREATHLESS

Words & Music by R.J. Lange, Andrea Corr, Caroline Corr, Sharon Corr & Jim Corr

1. The day-light's fad-ing slow-ly,
(Verse 2 see block lyric)
but time with you is stand-ing still. I'm wait-ing for
you on-ly, the slight-est touch and I feel weak.
I can-not lie, from you I can-not hide.

And I'm los - ing the will to try.
D.%. (I've lost my)

Can't hide it, can't fight it. So

go on, go on, come on, leave me breath - less.

Tempt me, tease me un - til I can't de - ny this

E
Aadd9
B
To Coda
lov - ing feel - ing. Make me long for your kiss.
E
Aadd9
1.
B
N.C.
Go on, go on. Yeah, come on.
Drums
2.
B
N.C.
B
come on.
F♯
C♯m
fr4
Yeah, yeah.

leave me breath - less._____ Go_____ on,_____ go_____ on,_____

_____ come on, leave me breath - less._____ Go_____ on,_____ go_____ on.

Verse 2:
And if there's no tomorrow
And all we have is here and now
I'm happy just to have you
You're all the love I need somehow
It's like a dream
Although I'm not asleep
And I never want to wake up
Don't lose it, don't leave it.

So go on, go on *etc.*

DANCING IN THE MOONLIGHT
Words & Music by Sherman Kelly

most ev - 'ry night _____ and when that _____ moon

_____ is _____ big _____ and _____ bright _____ it's a su - per - na - tu - ral _____ de - light. _____

_____ Ev - 'ry - bo - dy's danc - ing _____ in _____ the moon - light. _____ Danc-

- ing in the moon - light. _____ Ev - 'ry - bo - dy's _____ feel -

38

Bb/D   Cm   Cm/Bb   Fm9   Bb

-ing warm and bright, it's such a fine and na-tural sight.

Eb   Bb/D   Cm   Cm/Bb   *Repeat ad lib. to fade*

Ev-'ry-bo-dy's danc-ing in the moon-light. Danc-

Verse 3:
We like our fun and we never fight
You can't dance and stay uptight
It's a supernatural delight
Everybody was dancing in the moonlight.

Dancing in the moonlight *etc.*

COMING AROUND

Words & Music by Fran Healy

1. Moth-ers see it com-ing a-round,— (Verse 2 see block lyric) they know— they've got their

heads screwed— on.— I'm stand-ing in the mid-dle of town,—

I know— I might nev-er come home.— 'Cos stand-ing where I am with all— the

people pass-ing by me, and the sound of all— these pass-ers-by mixed

in with the bus and mo-tor-car,— I must— be sure these are the signs— cos I've—

— been here a mil-lion times— be-fore.   Just tell me when it's

com-ing a-round,— com-ing a-round.—

I think I see it com-ing to town,_____ hunt-ing me down,
(% drag-ging)

bring-ing me round._____
(2° & % com-ing a - round.)

To Coda ⊕

Ooh._____

Ooh.

Just tell me when it's

com - ing a - round,

com - ing a - round.

I think I see it com - ing to town,

drag - ging me down.

Just tell me when it's

D.%. al Coda

⊕ Coda

Verse 2:
Tell me if I'm bringing you down
Cos I was fine till you came along
You tell me they're the tears of a clown (clown)
That I'm confusing by abusing my mind
So far away I wanna to be
It's not so close to you and me
The things they call our destiny
Now why do you have to pick on me at all?
My walls are coming down.

Just tell me when *etc.*

I'M OUTTA LOVE

Words & Music by Anastacia, Sam Watters & Louis Biancaniello

Seems like my time___ has come and now___ I'm mov - in' on.___

___ And I'll be strong - er. *(Vocal ad lib.)*

I'm out - ta love___ set___ me free___

___ and let me out___ this mi - se - ry.___

___ Show me the way___ to get___ my life___

Drums

Drums

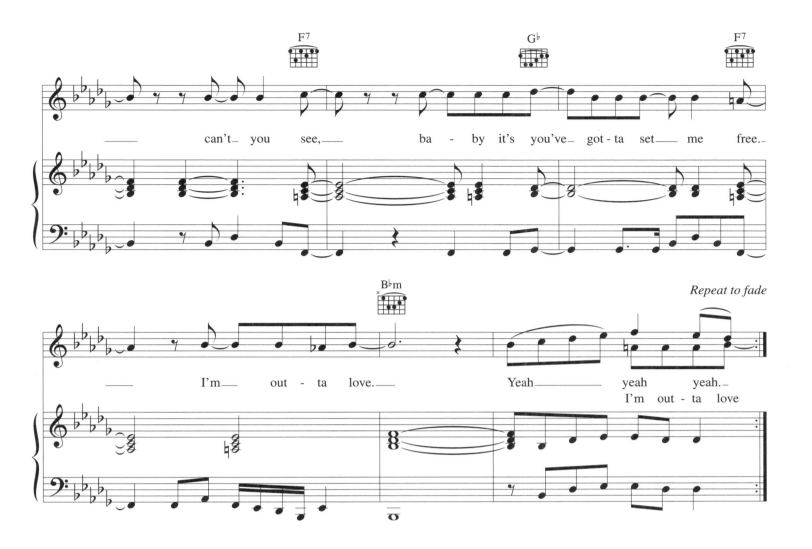

can't you see,___ ba-by it's you've_ got-ta set_ me free._

I'm_ out-ta love._ Yeah____ yeah yeah._

Repeat to fade

I'm out-ta love

Verse 2:
Said how many times
Have I tried to turn this love around
But every time
You just let me down
Come on be a man about it
You'll survive
Sure that you can work it out alright
Tell me yesterday did you know
I'd be the one to let you go?
And you know.

I'm outta love *etc.*

IT FEELS SO GOOD

Words & Music by Sonique, Linus Burdick & Simon Belofsky

what takes me high. (High-er than I've been be-

-fore.) Your love it keeps me a-live.

(Thought I should let you know.) That your touch, it means so

much. (When I'm a-lone at night) it's you

To Coda ⊕

I'm al-ways think-in' of. _____ Ooh, _____ ba - by.

1. Fm   D♭/F

B♭/F   D♭/F

2. Fm   D♭/F

Verse 2:
Ooh, I want you to understand how I feel, yeah, deep inside
Oh, you made me feel what I need to feel, yes, in my heart.

(Your love, it feels so good) *etc.*

KIDS

Words & Music by Robbie Williams & Guy Chambers

don't   mind   do-in' it   for   the   kids._____   (So   come on)

jump   on board,   take a ride,_____   (yeah

_____).   (You'll be doin' it all right.)   Jump   on   board,   feel the high

yeah,_____   'cause the kids are al - right.

Ooh ooh.—

2.

I'm gon-na give it all— of my lov - ing, it's gon-na take up all— of my love.

I'm gon-na give it all— of my lov - ing, it's gon-na take up all— of my love.

I'm gon-na give it all— of my lov - ing, it's gon-na take up all— of my love.

Come down from the ceil - ing I did-n't mean to get so high. I could-n't

do what I want-ed to do when my lips were dry. You

can't just up and leave me, I'm a sing-er in a band. Well

I like drum-mers ba - by, you're not my bag.

single hand-ed-ly rais-ing the e-con-o-my, ain't no chance of the re-cord com-pa-ny drop-ping me.
I've been look-ing for se-ri-al mo-no-ga-my, not some bird that looks like Bil-ly Con-nol-ly.

But for now, I'm down for or-ni-tho-lo-gy, grab your bi-no-cu-lars, come fol-low me.

I like to drink it up but nev-er like to sink it, uh, uh. I like to drink it up but nev-er like to sink it, uh, uh.

Repeat ad lib. to fade

I like to drink it up but nev-er like to sink it, uh, uh. Uh uh uh, uh uh uh, uh uh uh, uh uh uh.

LIFE IS A ROLLERCOASTER

Words & Music by Gregg Alexander & Rick Nowels

ba - by,_____
(Verse 2 see block lyric)

you real - ly got my tail in a spin.—

Hey— ba - by,_____

I don't ev - en know

where to be - gin.—

But ba - by I got— one—

— thing I want— you to know,—

wher -

66

Verse 2:
Hey Baby, you've really got me flying tonight
Hey Sugar, you almost got us punched in a fight
But Baby you know the one thing I gotta know
Wherever you go, tell me cos I'm gonna show.

We found love *etc.*

NATURAL BLUES

Words by Vera Hall
Music by Vera Hall & Moby
'Natural Blues' is based on the song 'Trouble So Hard' (Words & Music by Vera Hall)

MY LOVE

Words & Music by Jörgen Elofsson, Pelle Nylén, David Kreuger & Per Magnusson

1. An emp-ty street,_ an emp-ty house,_ a hole in-side_ my heart._ I'm

(Verse 2 see block lyric)

all a-lone,_ the rooms are get-ting small-er. I won-der how,_ I won-der why,_ I

Verse 2:
I try to read, I go to work
I'm laughing with my friends
But I can't stop to keep myself from thinking oh no,
I wonder how, I wonder why
I wonder where they are
The days we had
The songs we sang together, oh yeah.

And oh, my love *etc.*

PLEASE FORGIVE ME

Words & Music by David Gray

1. Please for-give me if I act a lit-tle strange,
(Verses 2, 3 & 4 see block lyrics)

for I know not what I do.

Feels— like light - ning run - ning through— my veins—

ev - 'ry - time— I look— at you,

ev - 'ry - time— I— look at

1-3.

you.

Verse 2:
Help me out here, all my words are falling short
And there's so much I want to say
Want to tell you just how good it feels
When you look at me that way
Ah, when you look at me that way.

Verse 3:
Throw a stone and watch the ripples flow
Moving out across the bay
Like a stone, I fall into your eyes
Deep into that mystery
Ah, deep into some mystery.

Verse 4:
I got half a mind to scream out loud
I got half a mind to die
So I won't ever have to lose you, girl
Won't ever have to say goodbye
I won't ever have to lie
Won't ever have to say goodbye.

OOPS!... I DID IT AGAIN
Words & Music by Max Martin & Rami

86

Verse 2:
You see my problem is this
I'm dreaming away
Wishing that heroes they truly exist
I cry watching the days
Can't you see I'm a fool in so many ways
But to lose all my senses
That is just so typically me.

Oops! I did it again *etc.*

PURE AND SIMPLE

Words & Music by Tim Hawes, Pete Kirtley & Alison Clarkson

92

Verse 2:
I'll be there through the stormiest weather
Always trying to make things a bit better
And I know I gotta try and get through to you
You can love me in a way like no other
But the situation's taking you under
So you need to tell me now what you wanna do.

I know I've been walking around in a daze (Baby, baby)
You gotta believe me when I say (Ah, ooh, ooh)

Wherever you go *etc.*

PURE SHORES

Words & Music by William Orbit & Shaznay Lewis

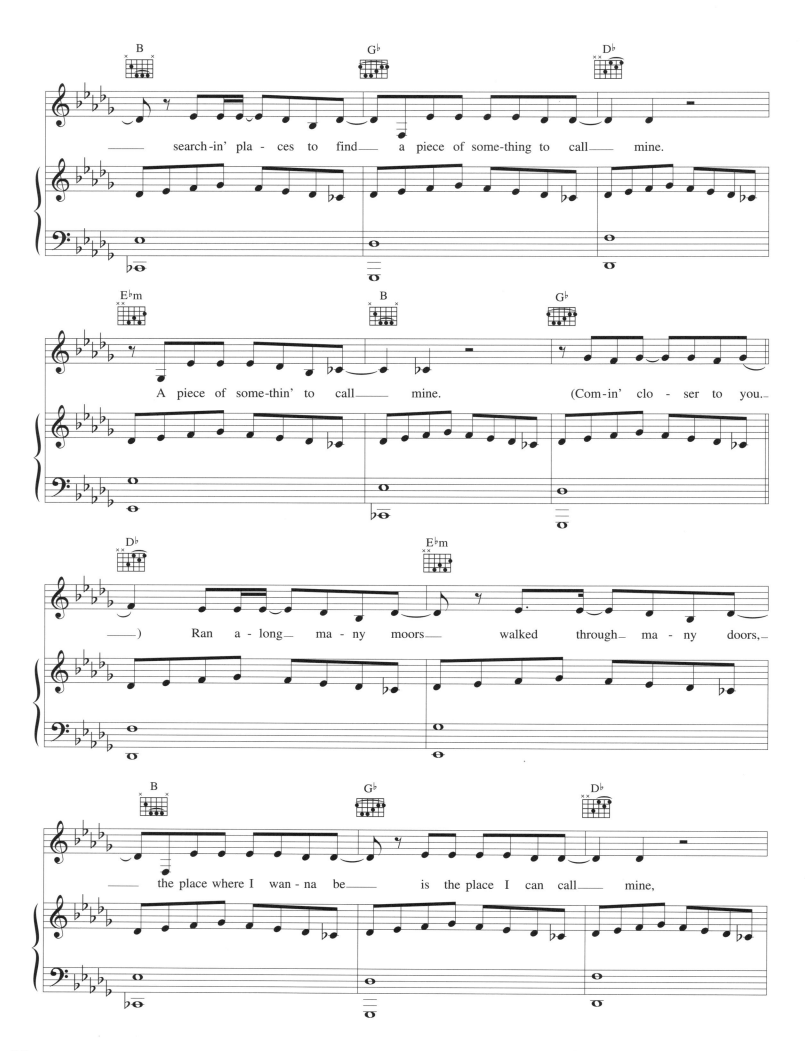

E♭m
B
G♭
- ing you,_ swim-ming clo - ser to_ you.
D♭
E♭m
Ma-ny fa - ces I_ have seen,_ ma-ny pla - ces I_ have been,_
B
G♭
_ walked the des - ert swam_ the shores._ (Com-in' clo - ser to you._
D♭
E♭m
) Ma - ny fa - ces I have known,_ ma - ny ways_ in which_ I've grown,_

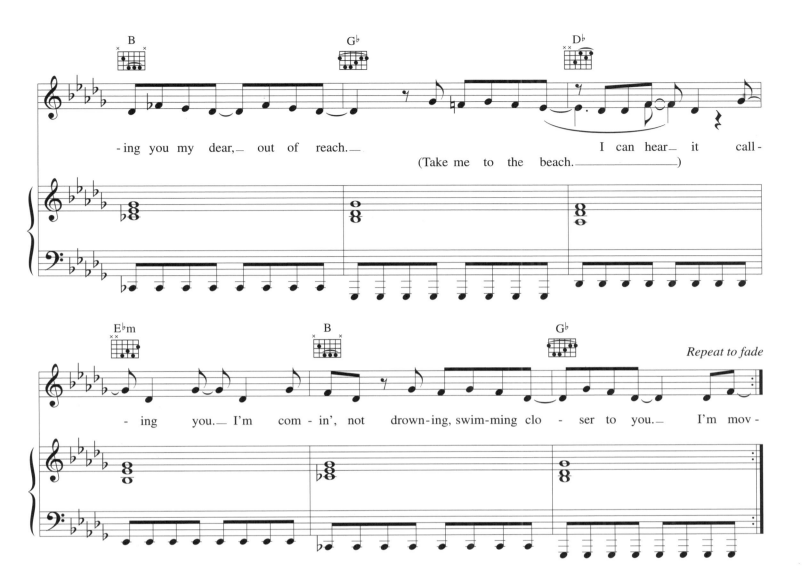

Verse 2:
Never been here before
I'm intrigued, I'm unsure
I'm searching for more
I've got something that's all mine
I've got something that's all mine.

Take me somewhere I can breathe
I've got so much to see
This is where I wanna be
In a place I can call mine
In a place I can call mine.

I'm movin' *etc.*

REACH

Words & Music by Cathy Dennis & Andrew Todd

me so **(F)** reach for the stars._ Climb ev - 'ry moun-

- tain high - er. Reach for the stars._ Fol - low_ your heart's

_ de - sire._ Reach for the stars._ And when_ that rain-

- bow's shin - ing ov - er you,_ that's when your dreams

107

RISE

Words & Music by Bob Dylan, Gabrielle, Ferdy Unger-Hamilton & Ollie Dagois

hopes, look at my dreams, I'm build-ing bridg-es from the scenes. Now I'm

rea - dy to rise a - gain. (Mm

1.

2.

) 3. Much time has passed be - tween us, mm,

do you still think of me at all? My world of bro-ken

pro-mis-es___ where you won't catch me when__ I fall.___ Look at my

life, look in my heart, I have seen them fall__ a - part.___ Now I'm

rea - dy___ to rise a - gain.___ Just look at my

hopes, look at my dreams, I'm build - ing bridg - es from__ the scenes.___ Now I'm

Verse 2:
Caught up in my thinking
Like a prisoner in my mind
You pose so many questions
That the truth is hard to find
I'd better think twice I know
That I'll get over you.

Look at my life *etc.*

ROCK DJ

Words & Music by Robbie Williams, Guy Chambers, Kelvin Andrews, Nelson Pigford & Ekundayo Paris

1. Me with the floor-show, kick-in' with your tor - so. Boys get-ting high and the girls ev - en more so.
(Verse 2 see block lyric)

Wave your hands if you're not with the man. Can I kick it? (Yes you can.)

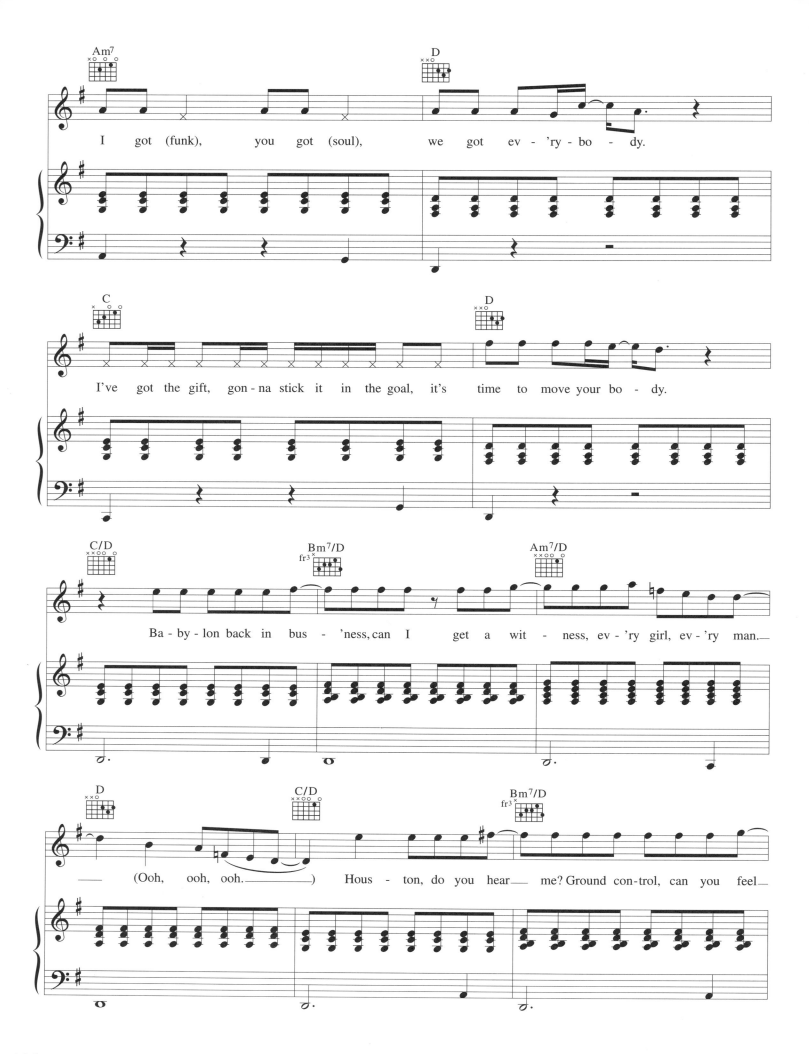

I got (funk), you got (soul), we got ev-'ry-bo - dy.

I've got the gift, gon-na stick it in the goal, it's time to move your bo - dy.

Ba - by - lon back in bus - 'ness, can I get a wit - ness, ev-'ry girl, ev-'ry man. __

__ (Ooh, ooh, ooh. __) Hous - ton, do you hear __ me? Ground con-trol, can you feel __

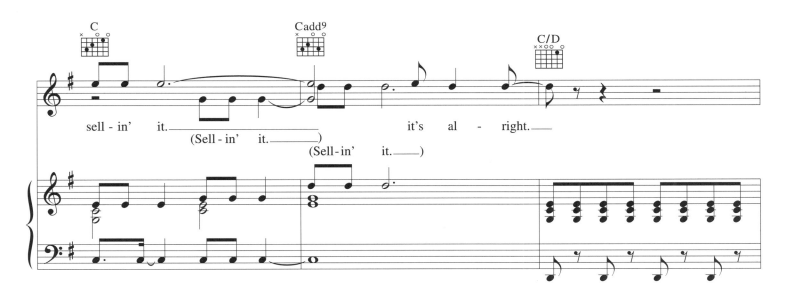

sell - in' it. _____ it's al - right. ____
(Sell - in' it. _____)
(Sell-in' it. ____)

D.%. *(Repeat chorus to fade)*

Come on!   I don't wan - na

Verse 2:
Singin' in the classes
Music for the masses
Give no head no backstage passes
Have a proper giggle
I'll be quite polite
But when I rock the mic, I rock the mic (right)
You got no love then you're with the wrong man
It's time to move your body
If you can't get a girl but your best friend can
It's time to move your body.

I don't wanna be sleazy
Baby, just tease me
Got no family planned
Houston, do you hear me?
Ground-control, can you feel me?
Need permission to land.

I don't wanna rock *etc.*

STAN

Words & Music by Marshall Mathers, Dido Armstrong & Paul Herman

It re-minds me that it's not so bad. It's not so bad.

Repeat 1º only

VERSE

(Verses 1 - 4 see block lyric)

Verse 1:
Dear Slim, I wrote you but you still ain't callin'
I left my cell, my pager, and my home phone at the bottom
I sent two letters back in autumn
You must not have got 'em
It probably was a problem at the post office or somethin'.

Sometimes I scribble addresses too sloppy when I jot 'em
But anyways, fuck it, what's been up man, how's your daughter?
My girlfriends pregnant too, I'm out to be a father
If I have a daughter, guess what I'm-a call her?
I'm-a name her Bonnie.

I read about your uncle Ronnie too, I'm sorry
I had a friend kill himself over some bitch who didn't want him.
I know you probably hear this everyday
But I'm your biggest fan.
I even got the underground shit that you did with Scam.

I got a room full of your posters and your pictures, man.
I like the shit you did with Ruckus too, that shit was fat.
Anyways, I hope you get this man
Hit me back, just to chat
Truly yours, your biggest fan, this is Stan.

Chorus

Verse 2:
Dear Slim, you still ain't called or wrote, I hope you have the chance
I ain't mad, I just think it's fucked up you don't answer fans.
If you didn't want to talk to me outside the concert, you didn't have to.
But you could have signed an autograph for Matthew.
That's my little brother, man. He's only 6 years old.
We waited in the blistering cold for you for 4 hours and ya just said no.
That's pretty shitty man, you're like his fuckin' idol
He wants to be just like you man, he likes you more than I do.

I ain't that mad, though I just don't like being lied to.
Remember when we met in Denver, you said if I write you
You would write me back. See, I'm just like you in a way.
I never knew my father neither.
He used to always cheat on my mom and beat her.

I can relate to what you're sayin' in your songs.
So when I have a shitty day, I drift away and put 'em on.
'Cause I don't really got shit else, so that shit helps when I'm depressed.
I even got a tattoo with your name across the chest.

Sometimes I even cut myself to see how much it bleeds.
It's like adrenaline. The pain is such a sudden rush for me.
See, everything you say is real, and I respect you cos you tell it.
My girlfriend's jealous 'cause I talk about you 24/7.
But she don't know you like I know you, Slim, no one does.
She don't know what it was like for people like us growing up.
You've gotta call me man. I'll be the biggest fan you'll ever lose.
Sincerely yours, Stan. PS: We should be together too.

Chorus

Verse 3:
Dear Mr. "I'm too good to call or write my fans."
This'll be the last package I ever send your ass.
It's been six months and still no word. I don't deserve it?
I know you got my last two letters, I wrote the addresses on 'em perfect.

So this is my cassette I'm sending you. I hope you hear it.
I'm in the car right now. I'm doing 90 on the freeway.
Hey Slim, "I drank a fifth of vodka, ya dare me to drive?"
You know that song by Phil Collins from "The Air In The Night?"
About that guy who could have saved that other guy from drowning?
But didn't? Then Phil saw it all then at his show he found him?
That's kinda how this is. You could have rescued me from drowning.
Now it's too late. I'm on a thousand downers now. I'm drowsy.

And all I wanted was a lousy letter or a call.
I hope you know I ripped all o' your pictures off the wall.
I love you Slim, we could have been together. Think about it.
You ruined it now, I hope you can't sleep and you dream about it.
And when you dream, I hope you can't sleep and you scream about it.
I hope your conscious eats at you and you can't breathe without me.
See Slim, (screaming) shut up bitch, I'm trying to talk.
Hey Slim, that's my girlfriend screaming in the trunk.
But I didn't slit her throat, I just tied her up,
See I ain't like you. 'Cause if she suffocates, she'll suffer more
And then she'll die too.
Well, gotta go, I'm almost at the bridge now.
Oh shit, I forgot, how am I supposed to send this shit out?

Section 1

Chorus

Verse 4:
Dear Stan, I meant to write you sooner, but I've just been busy.
You said your girlfriend's pregnant now, how far along is she?
Look, I'm really flattered you would call your daughter that.
And here's an autograph for your brother: I wrote it on your Starter cap.

I'm sorry I didn't see you at the show, I must have missed you.
Don't think I did that shit intentionally, just to diss you.
And what's this shit you said about you like to cut your wrists too?
I say that shit just clownin' dawg, c'mon, how fucked up is you?
You got some issues, Stan, I think you need some counsellin'
To help your ass from bouncin' off the walls when you get down some.

And what's this shit about us meant to be together?
That type of shit'll make me not want us to meet each other.
I really think you and your girlfriend need each other
Or maybe you just need to treat her better.
I hope you get to read this letter.
I just hope it reaches you in time.

Before you hurt yourself, I think that you'd be doin' just fine
If you'd relax a little, I'm glad that I inspire you, but Stan
Why are you so mad? Try to understand that I do want you as a fan.
I just don't want you to do some crazy shit.
I seen this one shit on the news a couple weeks ago that made me sick.
Some dude was drunk and drove his car over a bridge
And had his girlfriend in the trunk and she was pregnant with his kid.
And in the car they found a tape but it didn't say who it was to.
Come to think about it... his name was... it was you.

Damn.

SUNDAY MORNING CALL

Words & Music by Noel Gallagher

Dm   D

But what for?_____   And in____ your___ head___

§ G   D   Em⁷

_____ do you feel_____   what you're not_____ sup-posed____ to feel?_

C   G   D

_____ And you take_____   what you want,____   but you don't
(won't_

F   Em   D   G

_____) get it____ for free.____ §(hope_)   You need_____   more time_

124

coz your thoughts___ and words___ won't last_____ for - ev - er - more.___

To Coda ⊕

And I'm not sure_____ if it - 'll ev - - er work___ out right.

But it's O. K.___ It's al - right.

Con pedale

1. **2.**

Guitar

And in your head

Verse 2:
When you're lonely and you start to hear
The little voices in your head at night
You will only sniff away the tears
So you can dance until the morning light
At what price?

And in your head *etc.*

127

WALKING AWAY

Words & Music by Craig David & Mark Hill

from the trou- bles in___ my life.___ I'm walk-ing a- way,

oh,___ to find a bet- ter day.___ I'm walk-ing a- way___

from the trou- bles in___ my life.___ I'm walk-ing a- way___

oh,___ to find a bet- ter day.___ I'm walk-ing a- way.___

Verse 2:

Well I'm, so tired baby

Things you say, you're driving me away

Whispers in the powder room baby, don't listen to the games they play

Girl I thought you'd realise, I'm not like them other guys

Cos I say them with my own eyes, you should've been more wise, and

Well I don't wanna live my life, too many sleepless nights

Not mentioning the fights, I'm sorry to say lady.

I'm walking away *etc.*

WHAT MAKES A MAN

Words & Music by Steve Mac & Wayne Hector

and cry when you're a - part.__ If you know what makes_ a man

want to love you the way_ I do,__ girl, you got-ta let me_ know_____

1.
so I can get ov - er you.__ 2. What makes her_ so right_

2.
_ Oh.____ Oth - er girls_ will come_ a - long,_ they

Verse 2:
What makes her so right
Is it the sound of her laugh
That look in her eyes
When do you decide
She is the dream that you see
That force in your life
When you apologize no matter who was wrong
When you get on your knees if that would bring her home.

Tell me what makes a man *etc.*

YELLOW

Words & Music by Guy Berryman, Jon Buckland, Will Champion & Chris Martin

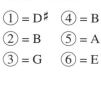

Guitar Tuned:

① = D♯   ④ = B
② = B   ⑤ = A
③ = G   ⑥ = E

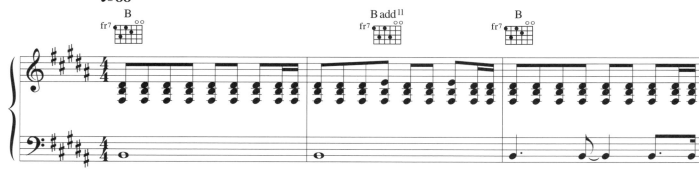

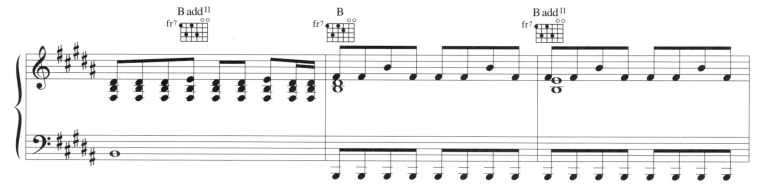

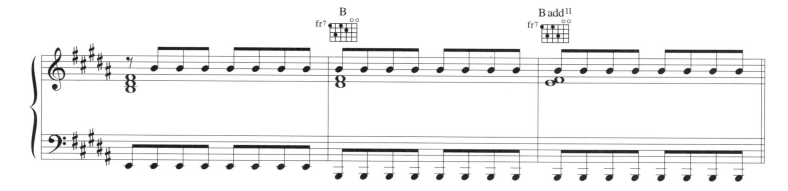

Verse 2:
I swam across, I jumped across for you
Oh, what a thing to do
'Cause you were all yellow
I drew a line, I drew a line for you
Oh, what a thing to do
And it was all yellow.

Your skin, oh yeah, your skin and bones
Turn into something beautiful
And you know, for you I'd bleed myself dry
For you I'd bleed myself dry.

Exclusive distributors:
Music Sales Limited
8/9 Frith Street,
London W1V 5TZ, England.
Music Sales Pty Limited
120 Rothschild Avenue
Rosebery, NSW 2018,
Australia.

Order No.AM970860
ISBN 0-7119-8910-9
This book © Copyright 2001 by Wise Publications

Cover design by Chloë Alexander

Printed in Malta by Interprint Ltd.

Your Guarantee of Quality
As publishers, we strive to produce every book to the highest
commercial standards. The music has been freshly engraved and
the book has been carefully designed to minimise awkward page
turns and to make playing from it a real pleasure. Particular care
has been given to specifying acid-free, neutral-sized paper made
from pulps which have not been elemental chlorine bleached.
This pulp is from farmed sustainable forests and was produced
with special regard for the environment. Throughout, the printing
and binding have been planned to ensure a sturdy, attractive
publication which should give years of enjoyment. If your copy
fails to meet our high standards, please inform us and we will
gladly replace it.

Music Sales' complete catalogue describes thousands of titles
and is available in full colour sections by subject, direct from
Music Sales Limited. Please state your areas of interest and send
a cheque/postal order for £1.50 for postage to: Music Sales
Limited, Newmarket Road, Bury St. Edmunds, Suffolk IP33 3YB.

www.musicsales.com